SO-APP-352

Pre-k. 2548 E
A

THE SHEPHERD

This translation first published
in the United States of America in 1967.
Originally published in Switzerland in 1966 under the title *Der Hirte*.
L.C. Card 67-18394
Printed in Switzerland

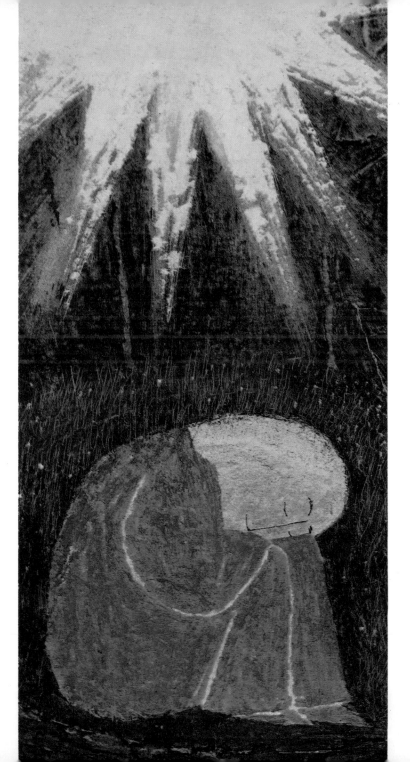

THE SHEPHERD

By Helga Aichinger

Thomas Y. Crowell Company   New York

Illustrations copyright © 1966 by Neugebauer Press, Bad Goisern, Austria, and Nord-Sud Verlag, Monchaltorf, Switzerland. All rights reserved.

Once upon a time there was an old shepherd who lived on the side of a mountain. While his sheep grazed, he played his flute.

The shepherd was poor and lonely. The only house on the mountain was his old hut. A narrow path led to it.

One night, when the shepherd was sleeping under the palm trees, he had a dream. A great shining star appeared in the sky. He had never seen a star as beautiful as this. And an angel came to him and said: "Fear not, I bring joyful news. On this night the Christ Child is born. Wake up and follow the star!"

The shepherd woke up. There, above him in the sky, was the great shining star. The angel had flown away, but he could still see the brightness where he had been.

So the shepherd awakened his sheep, and he took his staff and his flute, and followed the star. Across the valleys and the mountains he followed it, and the sheep followed him.

They came to a beautiful town. The shepherd thought: I might find the Christ Child here. But the star led him on.

They came to a magnificent castle. Again the shepherd thought:
I shall find the Christ Child here. But still the star led him on.

They came to a lonely field. There stood an old hut with a narrow path leading to it. The shepherd started to turn back. He thought he had lost his way. But the star dipped down and stood still over the hut.

The old shepherd's eyes opened with wonder. There was the Child lying on straw and hay in the manger. Mary and Joseph had fallen asleep, but the Child gazed at the shepherd, and he knelt in awe.

"You are the Christ Child," the shepherd said, "but you are so poor. You have no cradle and you have to sleep in a manger on straw and hay."

He took off his coat to cover the little boy.

Then the Christ Child smiled at him, and the old shepherd knew the Christ Child was not poor at all. "Heaven and earth belong to you," he said.

FIRST METH. CHURCH
LIBRARY
DELMAR, N. Y.